Pick up a few pre-cuts of colorful fabrics and let the fu
The seven designs in this book are all small projects that you ca

LEISURE ARTS, INC. • Maumelle, Arkansas

wild goose chase TABLE RUNNER

Finished Table Runner Size: 14 1/4" x 42 1/2"
(36 cm x 108 cm)
Finished Block Size: 10" x 10" (25 cm x 25 cm)

SHOPPING LIST

Yardage is based on 43"/44" (109 cm/112 cm) wide fabric with a usable width of 40" (102 cm). Fat quarters are approximately 18" x 21" (46 cm x 53 cm).

- ☐ 3 assorted blue fat quarters
- ☐ 3 assorted green fat quarters
- ☐ 1 green fat quarter for setting triangles
- ☐ 23" x 52" (58 cm x 132 cm) piece of batting
- ☐ 1 1/2 yds (1.4 m) of white solid fabric for backing
- ☐ 1 3/8 yds (1.3 m) of fabric for lining

CUTTING THE PIECES

*Follow **Rotary Cutting**, page 26, to cut fabric. For fat quarters, cut all strips parallel to the long edge of the fabric. The setting triangles are cut slightly larger and will be trimmed after stitching. All measurements include 1/4" seam allowances.*

From *each* of 3 assorted blue fat quarters:

- Cut 3 strips 3" wide. From these strips, cut 16 **squares** 3" x 3".

From *each* of 3 assorted green fat quarters:

- Cut 3 strips 3" wide. From these strips, cut 8 **rectangles** 5 1/2" x 3".

From remaining green fat quarter:

- Cut 1 strip 15 1/2" wide. From this strip, cut 1 square 15 1/2" x 15 1/2". Cut this square ***twice*** diagonally to make 4 **setting triangles**.

From fabric for backing:

- Cut **backing** 23" x 52".

MAKING THE BLOCK

*Follow **Machine Sewing or Piecing**, page 27, and **Pressing**, page 28, to complete table runner. Match right sides and raw edges and use a 1/4" seam allowance throughout.*

1. Draw a diagonal line on wrong side of each **square**.
2. For 1 Block, select 16 **squares** from 1 fabric and 8 **rectangles** from 1 fabric.
3. Matching right sides, place 1 square on 1 end of 1 rectangle and stitch along drawn line ***(Fig. 1)***. Trim 1/4" from stitching line ***(Fig. 2)***; press open ***(Fig. 3)***.

Fig. 1

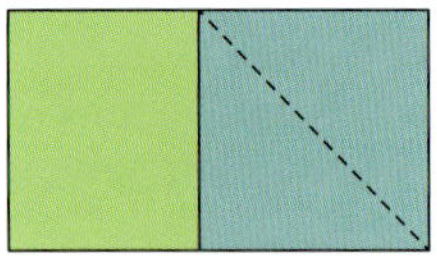

Fig. 2

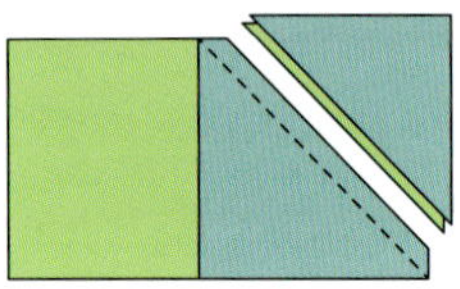

Fig. 3

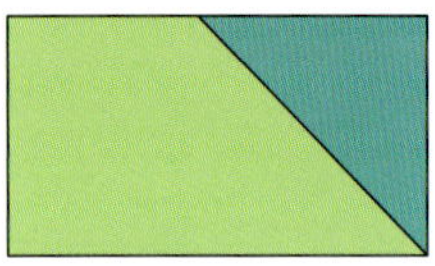

4. Place another square on opposite end of rectangle. Stitch and trim as before. Press open to make **Flying Geese Unit**. Make 8 matching Flying Geese Units.

Flying Geese Unit (make 8)

5. Sew 2 Flying Geese Units together to make **Unit 1**. Make 4 Unit 1's.

Unit 1 (make 4)

6. Sew 4 Unit 1's together to make **Block**. Block should measure 10 1/2" x 10 1/2" including seam allowances.

Block

7. Repeat Steps 2-6 to make a total of 3 Blocks.

ASSEMBLING THE TABLE RUNNER TOP

*Refer to **Assembly Diagram** to assemble table runner top.*

1. Aligning 1 edge, stitch 1 **setting triangle** and 1 **Block** together to make **Unit 2**. Make 2 Unit 1's. Press seam allowances toward triangles.

Unit 2 (make 2)

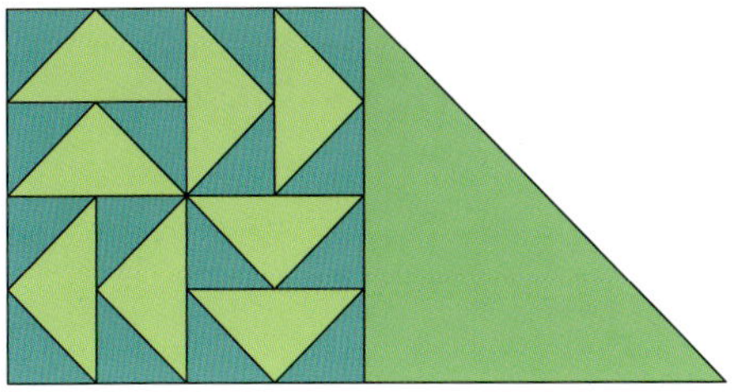

2. Aligning 1 edge, stitch setting triangles to opposite edges of 1 Block to make **Unit 3**. Press seam allowances toward triangles.

Unit 3

3. Nesting seam allowances, stitch the Units together to make Quilt Top.
4. Trim the setting triangles even with the Blocks.

Assembly Diagram

FINISHING THE TABLE RUNNER

1. Follow **Quilting**, page 28, to mark, layer, and quilt as desired. Our table runner is quilted with curved lines in and around the Flying Geese and an all-over swirl pattern in the setting triangles.
2. Trim batting and backing even with edges of table runner top.
3. To cut lining, place quilted table runner on lining fabric; trim around table runner edges.
4. Sew table runner and lining together, leaving an opening for turning. Turn right side out; press. Sew opening closed.

fabric-covered CANVASES

Finished Sizes:
Large - 12" x 24" (30 cm x 61 cm)
Medium - 11" x 14" (28 cm x 36 cm)
Small - 9" x 12" (23 cm x 30 cm)

SHOPPING LIST

Fat quarters are approximately 18" x 21" (46 cm x 53 cm).

- ☐ 12" x 24" x $^{5}/_{8}$" (30 cm x 61 cm x 16 mm) artist's canvas
- ☐ 11" x 14" x $^{5}/_{8}$" (28 cm x 36 cm x 16 mm) artist's canvas
- ☐ two 9" x 12" x $^{5}/_{8}$" (23 cm x 30 cm x 16 mm) artist's canvases
- ☐ 8 assorted fat quarters
- ☐ 32" x 45" (81 cm x 114 cm) piece of cotton batting
- ☐ staple gun and staples

CUTTING THE PIECES

*Follow **Rotary Cutting**, page 26, to cut fabric. All measurements include $^{1}/_{4}$" seam allowances.*

For large canvas:

- Cut **rectangle A** 15" x 18" from 1 fat quarter.
- Cut **rectangle B** 15" x 3$^{1}/_{2}$" from 1 fat quarter.
- Cut **rectangle C** 15" x 6$^{1}/_{2}$" from 1 fat quarter.
- Cut **batting** 15" x 27".

For medium canvas:

- Cut **rectangle D** 11" x 14" from 1 fat quarter.
- Cut **rectangle E** 14" x 6$^{1}/_{2}$" from 1 fat quarter.
- Cut **batting** 14" x 17".

For each small canvas:

- Cut **rectangle F** 12" x 11$^{1}/_{2}$".
- Cut **rectangle G** 12" x 4".
- Cut **batting** 12" x 15".

COVERING THE CANVASES

*Follow **Machine Sewing or Piecing**, page 27, and **Pressing**, page 28. Match right sides and raw edges and use a $^{1}/_{4}$" seam allowance throughout.*

1. For each canvas, sew corresponding **rectangles** together; press seam allowances toward darker fabric.
2. Center **batting** and pieced fabric over canvas. Beginning at center top and center bottom, staple fabric to back of canvas. Staple fabric to back of canvas at side centers.
3. Working top to bottom and side to side and mitering corners, pull fabric taut; staple fabric to back of canvas. **Tip:** When mitering the corners, it will be helpful to trim some of the fabric and batting bulk out of the corners.

tote BAG

Finished Size: 12"w x 14"h x 4"d (30 cm x 36 cm x 10 cm)

SHOPPING LIST

Yardage is based on 43"/44" (109 cm/112 cm) wide fabric with a usable width of 40" (102 cm). Fat quarters are approximately 18" x 21" (46 cm x 53 cm).

- ☐ 1 jelly roll or 40 assorted strips 2 1/2" x 40" (6 cm x 102 cm)
- ☐ 2 white solid fat quarters for backing
- ☐ 1/2 yd (46 cm) of fabric for lining
- ☐ 22" x 40" (56 cm x 102 cm) piece of cotton batting
- ☐ water-soluble fabric marking pen

CUTTING THE PIECES

*Follow **Rotary Cutting**, page 26, to cut fabric. For yardage, cut all strips from the selvage-to-selvage width of the fabric. All measurements include 1/4" seam allowances.*

From white solid fat quarters:

- Cut 2 **backings** 18" x 20".

From fabric for lining:

- Cut 1 strip 16 1/2" wide. From this strip, cut 2 **linings** 16 1/2" x 16 1/2".

From cotton batting:

- Cut 1 **handle strip** 1 1/4" x 40".
- Cut 2 **bodies** 18" x 20".

MAKING THE FRONT AND BACK

*Follow **Machine Sewing or Piecing**, page 27, and **Pressing**, page 28, to complete tote bag. Match right sides and raw edges and use a 1/4" seam allowance throughout.*

1. Set aside 1 jelly roll strip for handles, 1 jelly roll strip for handle linings, and 1 jelly roll strip for tote bag trims.
2. For tote bag front, refer to **Fig. 1** to draw a line through the center of 1 batting **body** and 1 line at a 45° angle 1 1/2" from bottom edge.

Fig. 1

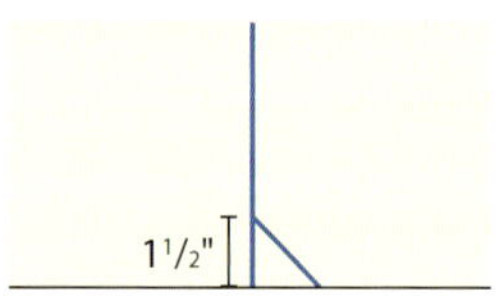

3. Layer 1 batting body on top of 1 **backing**. Referring to **Fig. 2**, place 1 strip, right side up, aligning 1 corner with vertical line and 1 long edge with diagonal line; pin.

Fig. 2

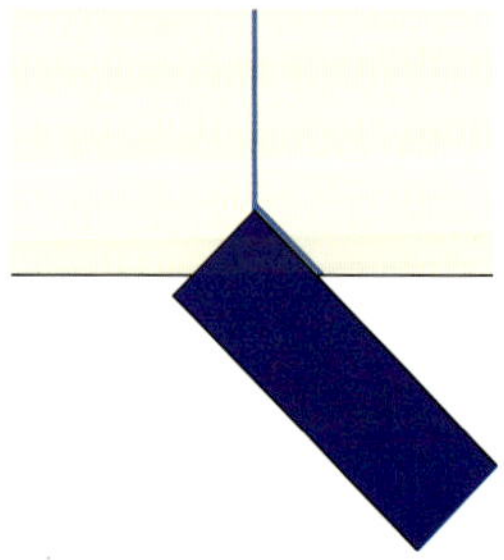

4. Matching raw edges, align another strip with previous strip; sew 1/4" from raw edge **(Fig. 3)**.

Fig. 3

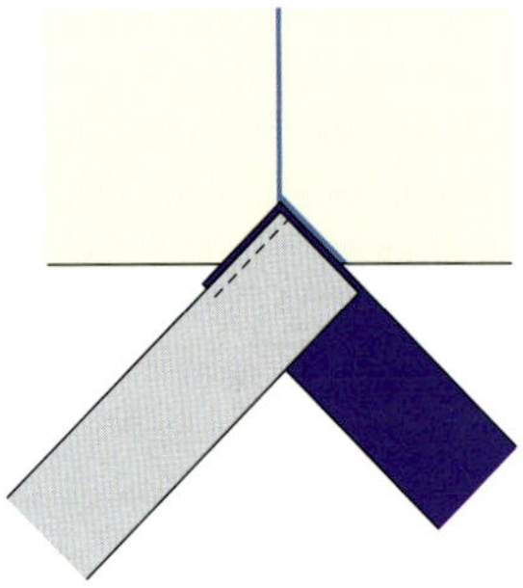

5. Press strip to right side. Trim strips slightly beyond batting edge **(Fig. 4)**.

Fig. 4

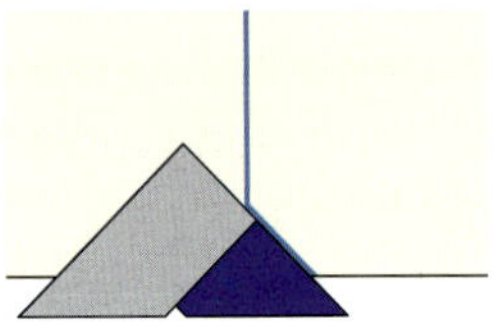

6. Matching raw edges, align another strip with previous strips; sew along raw edge **(Fig. 5)**.

Fig. 5

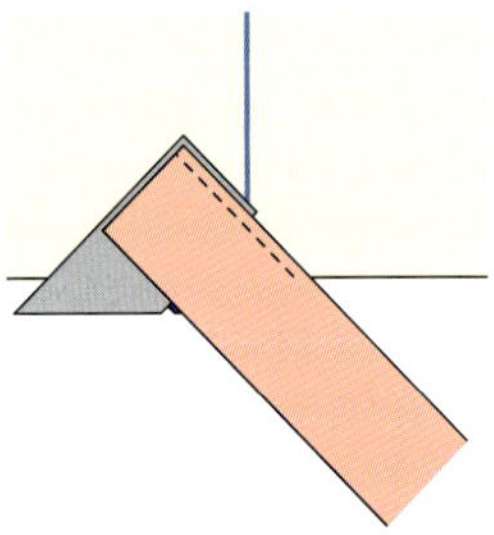

7. Press strip to right side **(Fig. 6)**. Trim strip slightly beyond batting edge.

Fig. 6

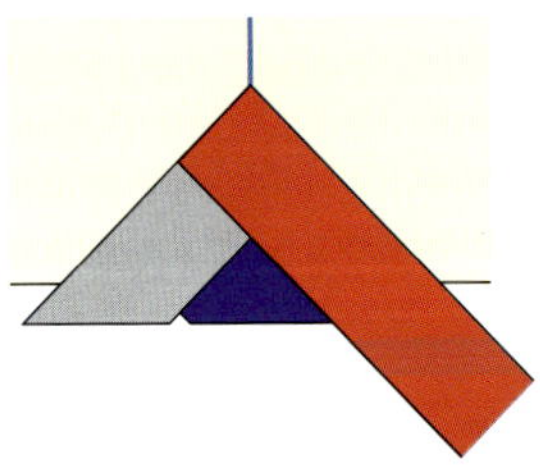

8. Repeat Steps 4-7 to add strips to cover remainder of batting, trimming strip ends slightly beyond batting edges **(Fig. 7)**.

Fig. 7

9. Repeat Steps 1-8 to make tote bag back.
10. For tote bag front and back, center a vertical row of points of strips and trim each piece to 16 1/2" x 16 1/2".
11. Cut tote bag trim strip in half.
12. Draw a line 2 1/8" from top edge of tote bag front. Align raw edge of 1 trim strip with drawn line; stitch 1/4" from raw edge **(Fig. 8)**. Press trim to right side. Baste along long raw edge **(Fig. 9)**.

Fig. 8

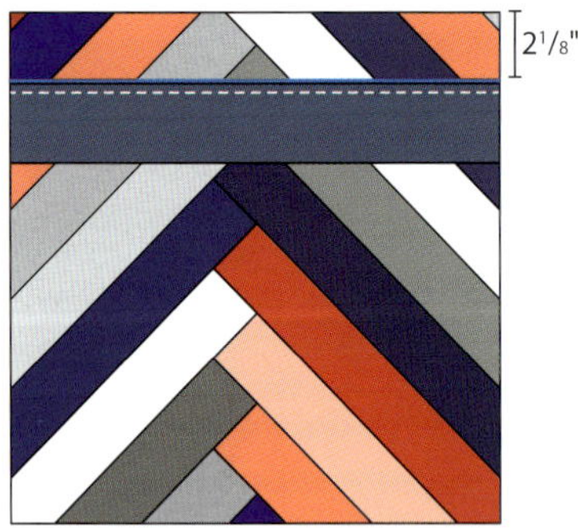

Fig. 9

13. Repeat Step 12 with remaining trim strip and tote bag back.

ASSEMBLING THE HANDLES

1. Sew handle strip to handle lining strip along 1 long raw edge. Press seam allowance toward lining strip.
2. Lay batting handle strip on handle lining strip along seamline **(Fig. 10)**.

Fig. 10

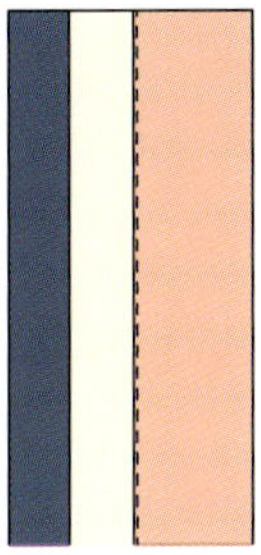

3. Press handle lining over batting **(Fig. 11)**.

Fig. 11

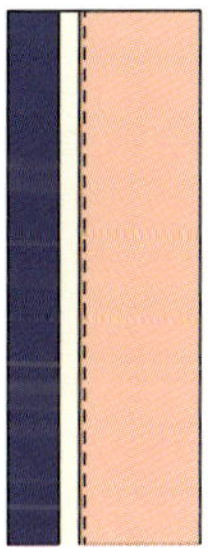

4. Folding raw edge under even with opposite edge of handle lining, press handle strip over batting; topstitch in place **(Fig. 12)**. Topstitch along opposite edge. Add topstitching as desired.

Fig. 12

5. Cut handle strip in half to make 2 handles.

ASSEMBLE THE TOTE BAG

1. Pin ends of 1 handle to tote bag front as shown in **Fig. 13**; baste.

Fig. 13

2. Repeat Step 1 to attach remaining handle to tote bag back.
3. With handles sandwiched in between, sew tote bag front to tote bag lining along top edge. Repeat with tote bag back and lining.
4. Matching right sides, place bag front and bag back together and linings together. Stitch along raw edges, leaving a 4" opening in bottom of linings to turn bag.
5. To box the bag front/bag back bottom, match right sides and align bag side seam with bottom seam. Refer to **Fig. 14** to sew across point 2" from end. Trim ¼" from seamline. Repeat for remaining end of bag front/bag back and lining front/lining back.

Fig. 14

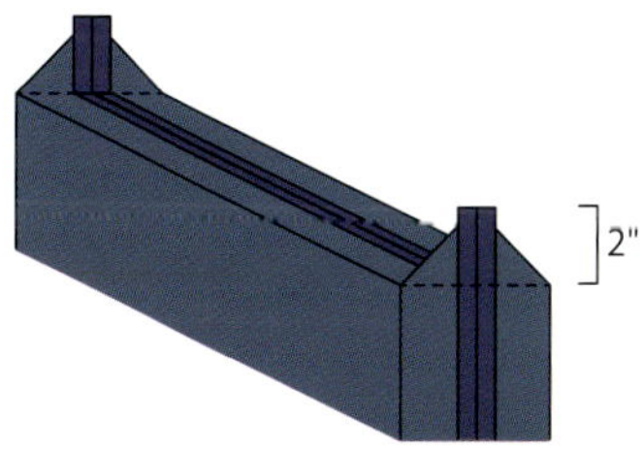

6. Turn bag right side out through opening; sew opening closed. Push lining into bag; press top edge. Topstitch around top edge of tote bag.

cathedral WINDOW PILLOW

Finished Pillow Size: 16" x 16" (41 cm x 41 cm)

SHOPPING LIST

Fat quarters are approximately 18" x 21" (46 cm x 53 cm).

- ☐ 4 green mottled print fat quarters
- ☐ 5 assorted print fat quarters
- ☐ 18" x 18" (46 cm x 46 cm) piece of muslin for pillow top backing
- ☐ 18" x 18" (46 cm x 46 cm) piece of batting
- ☐ 16" x 16" (41 cm x 41 cm) pillow form
- ☐ 1" (25 mm) safety pins

CUTTING THE PIECES

*Follow **Rotary Cutting**, page 26, to cut fabric. For fat quarters, cut all strips parallel to the long edge of the fabric. All measurements include $^{1}/_{4}$" seam allowances.*

From green mottled print fat quarters:

- Cut **pillow back** 16$^{1}/_{2}$" x 16$^{1}/_{2}$".
- Cut 8 strips 2$^{1}/_{2}$" wide. From these strips, cut 64 **background squares** 2$^{1}/_{2}$" x 2$^{1}/_{2}$".
- Cut 13 strips 2$^{1}/_{2}$" wide. From these strips, cut 100 **framing squares** 2$^{1}/_{2}$" x 2$^{1}/_{2}$".

From *each* assorted print fat quarter:

- Cut 1 strip 2$^{1}/_{2}$" wide. From this strip, cut 6 **middle squares** 2$^{1}/_{2}$" x 2$^{1}/_{2}$". (You will have extra squares. This will provide variety in your blocks.)

MAKING THE PILLOW

*Follow **Machine Sewing or Piecing**, page 27, and **Pressing**, page 28, to complete pillow. Match right sides and raw edges and use a $^{1}/_{4}$" seam allowance throughout.*

1. Press each **framing square** in half diagonally to make triangles.
2. Place 1 triangle on each **background square**. With triangles sandwiched in between, sew background squares together to make **Row 1**.

Row 1

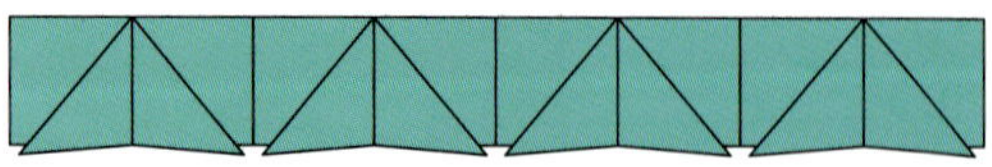

3. Place 1 triangle on each outer background square and 2 triangles on each inner background square. Pay close attention to the orientation of the triangles. With triangles sandwiched in between, sew background squares together to make **Row 2**. Repeat to make Row 4 and Row 6.

Rows 2, 4, & 6

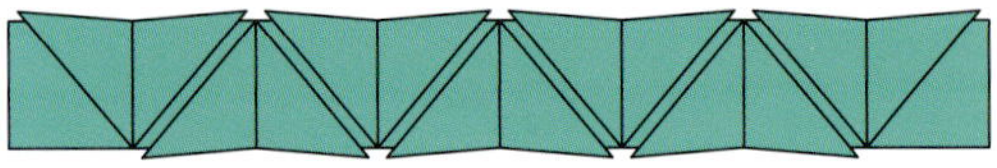

4. Place 1 triangle on each outer background square and 2 triangles on each inner background square. Pay close attention to the orientation of the triangles. With triangles sandwiched in between, sew background squares together to make **Row 3**. Repeat to make Row 5 and Row 7.

Rows 3, 5, & 7

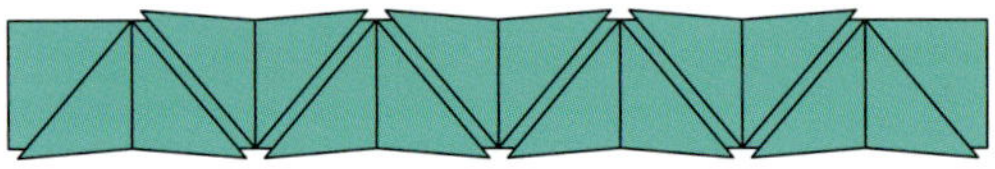

5. Place 1 triangle on each **background square**. With triangles sandwiched in between, sew background squares together to make **Row 8**.

Row 8

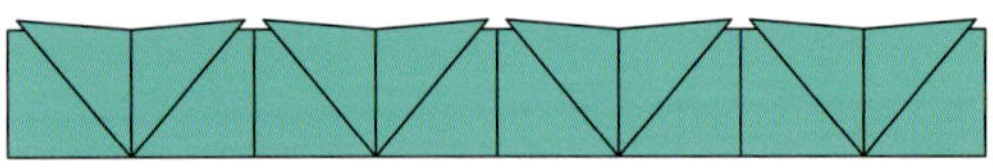

6. Paying close attention to the orientation of the triangles, sew Rows together to make **Unit 1**.

Unit 1

7. Layer pillow top backing, batting, and Unit 1.
8. Referring to **Fig. 1**, pin a **middle square** where 4 triangle points meet.

Fig. 1

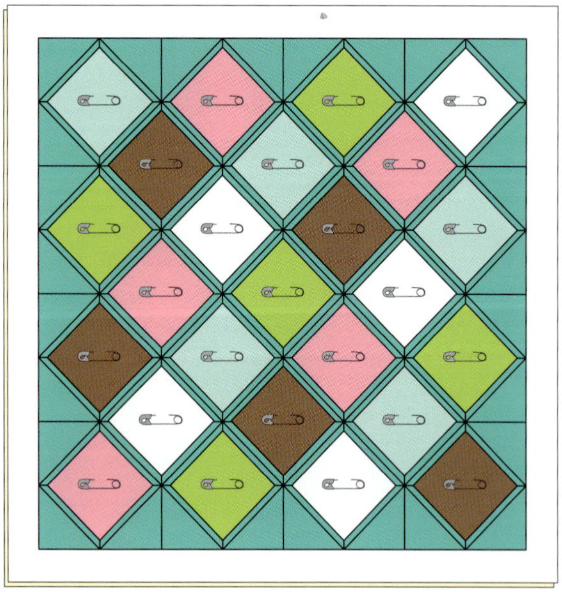

9. Refer to **Pillow Top Diagram** and fold 1 triangle edge over a middle square. Topstitch curved edge in place through all layers. Repeat with all triangle edges. You can fold and topstitch around 1 square at a time or you can pin all edges and topstitch in a random continuous path.

10. To complete pillow top, trim backing and batting even with edges of Unit 1.

11. Leaving an opening for turning, sew pillow top to **pillow back**. Insert pillow form in pillow; hand sew opening closed.

Pillow Top Diagram

ironing board CADDY

Finished Size: 9" x 30" (23 cm x 76 cm)
Fits ironing board 14" - 18" (36 cm - 46 cm) wide.

SHOPPING LIST

Fat quarters are approximately 18" x 21" (46 cm x 53 cm).

- ☐ 2 matching blue print fat quarters for caddy body and backing
- ☐ 3 assorted print fat quarters
- ☐ white solid fat quarter for pocket and pocket flap linings
- ☐ medium weight fusible interfacing
- ☐ 12" x 33" (30 cm x 84 cm) piece of cotton batting
- ☐ 6" (15 cm) of white ¾" (19 mm) sew-on hook and loop fastener
- ☐ ground walnut shells or ground emery for pincushion filling
- ☐ tracing paper

CUTTING THE PIECES

Follow ***Rotary Cutting****, page 26, to cut fabric. For fat quarters, cut all strips parallel to the long edge of the fabric. All measurements include ¼" seam allowances.*

From matching blue print fat quarters:

- Cut 2 strips 15½" wide. From these strips, cut 4 **body rectangles** 9½" x 15½".

From 1 print fat quarter:

- Cut **pocket** 9½" x 5½".
- Use pattern, page 18, to cut **pocket flap**.

From 1 print fat quarter:

- Cut **pocket** 9½" x 5½".

From 1 print fat quarter:

- Cut **pincushion** 8½" x 6".

From white solid fat quarter:

- Cut 2 **pocket linings** 9½" x 5½".
- Use pattern, page 18, to cut **pocket flap lining**

From interfacing:

- Cut **pincushion** 8½" x 6".

MAKING THE CADDY

*Follow **Machine Sewing or Piecing**, page 27, and **Pressing**, page 28, to complete caddy. Match right sides and raw edges and use a $^1/_4$" seam allowance throughout.*

1. For caddy body, sew 2 **body rectangles** together along 1 short edge; press seam allowances open. Repeat with remaining body rectangles to make caddy body lining.
2. Layer caddy body in center of batting. Quilt as desired. We stitched evenly spaced lines along the length of the caddy. Trim the batting even with the caddy body.
3. Center and sew hook side of hook and loop fastener over seamline on caddy body.
4. Sew **pocket** and **pocket lining** together along 1 long side; press with wrong sides together. Repeat with remaining pocket and pocket lining.
5. Aligning raw edges, baste 1 pocket to each end of caddy body.
6. Sew caddy body and caddy body lining together, leaving an opening along 1 long side for turning. Turn right side out; press. Sew opening closed.
7. Sew **pocket flap** and **pocket flap lining** together, leaving an opening along long straight edge for turning. Turn right side out; press. Sew opening closed.
8. Place top edge of pocket flap $5^1/_2$" from lower edge of caddy. Edge stitch and topstitch pocket flap in place.
9. On remaining pocket, stitch dividing lines as desired to hold sewing notions.
10. Follow manufacturer's instructions to fuse interfacing pincushion to wrong side of **pincushion**. Refer to **Fig. 1** to sew remaining piece of hook and loop fastener to pincushion.

Fig. 1

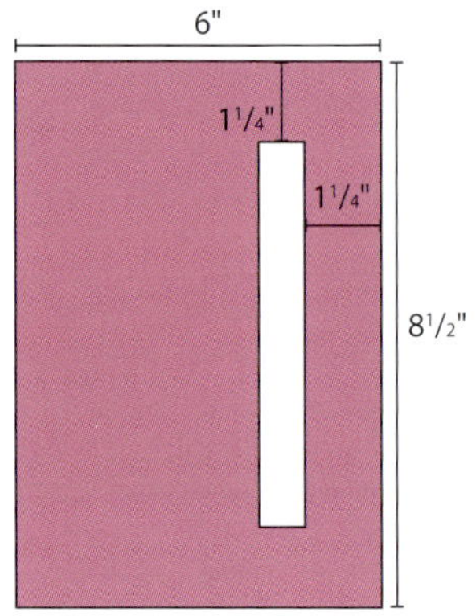

11. Matching long edges, fold pincushion in half and sew along raw edges, leaving an opening for turning. Turn right side out; press.
12. Fill pincushion with walnut shells or emery; sew opening closed.

Pocket Flap Pattern

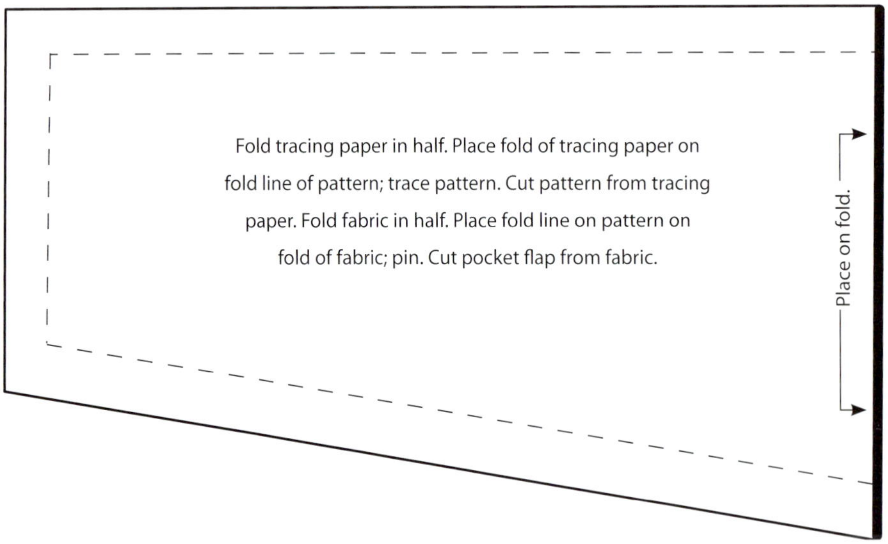

cosmetics BAG

Finished Size: 13" x 5" (33 cm x 13 cm)

SHOPPING LIST

Fat quarters are approximately 18" x 21" (46 cm x 53 cm).

- ☐ 1 fat quarter of purple print fabric
- ☐ 1 fat quarter of floral print fabric
- ☐ 1 fat quarter for lining
- ☐ 7 assorted fat quarters of print fabrics
- ☐ 14" x 17" (36 cm x 43 cm) piece of fusible fleece
- ☐ 16" (41 mm) polyester all-purpose zipper
- ☐ 5" (13 cm) of 1/4" (6 mm) double-face satin ribbon
- ☐ sewing machine zipper foot

CUTTING THE PIECES

*Follow **Rotary Cutting**, page 26, to cut fabric. For fat quarters, cut all strips parallel to the long edge of the fabric. All measurements include 1/4" seam allowances.*

From purple print fat quarter:

- Cut 2 strips 1 1/2" wide. From these strips, cut 2 **top strips** 1 1/2" x 15 1/2".

From floral print fat quarter:

- Cut 2 strips 2 1/4" wide. From these strips, cut 2 **bottom strips** 2 1/4" x 15 1/2".

From lining fat quarter:

- Cut 2 **lining pieces** 6 1/4" x 15 1/2".

From *each* assorted print fat quarter (including above):

- Cut 1 strip 2" wide. From each strip, cut 5 **squares** 2" x 2". (You will have extra squares. This will provide variety for your bag.)

From fusible fleece:

- Cut 2 **fleece pieces** 6 1/4" x 15 1/2".

MAKING THE BAG FRONT AND BACK

*Follow **Machine Sewing or Piecing**, page 27, and **Pressing**, page 28, to complete bag. Use a 1/4" seam allowance throughout.*

1. Sew 2 assorted **squares** together to make **Unit 1**. Make 20 Unit 1's. Sew 10 Unit 1's together to make **Unit 2**. Make 2 Unit 2's.

Unit 1 (make 20)

Unit 2 (make 2)

2. Sew 1 **top strip** and 1 **bottom strip** to 1 Unit 2 to make the **Bag Front**.

Bag Front

3. Repeat Step 2 to make the Bag Back.

ASSEMBLING THE BAG

1. Fuse 1 **fleece piece** to wrong side of 1 **lining piece**. Repeat with remaining fleece piece and lining piece.
2. Place the bag front, right side up, on a flat surface. Place 1 long edge of zipper, teeth side down, on top raw edge of bag front with zipper pull approximately 3/4" from short raw edge **(Fig. 1)**. Zipper tape ends may extend beyond opposite short raw edge; trim zipper tape ends even with edge.

Fig. 1

3. Place 1 long edge of lining piece, right side down, over the zipper. Moving zipper stop as needed, use zipper foot to sew 1/4" from zipper teeth through all layers **(Fig. 2)**.

Fig. 2

4. Repeat Steps 2-3 with bag back and remaining lining piece.
5. Open the zipper half way.
6. Matching right sides, place bag front and bag back together and linings together. Stitch along raw edges, leaving a 4" opening in bottom of linings to turn bag **(Fig. 3)**.

Fig. 3

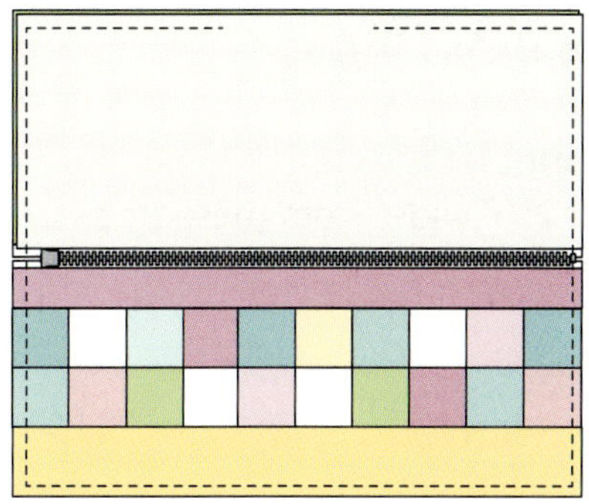

Note: *Previously sewn seam allowances on wrong side of bag front/back are not shown.*

7. To box the lining bottoms, match right sides and align lining side seam with bottom seam. Refer to **Fig. 4** to sew across point 1" from end. Trim 1/4" from seamline. Repeat for remaining end of lining and bag front/bag back.

Fig. 4

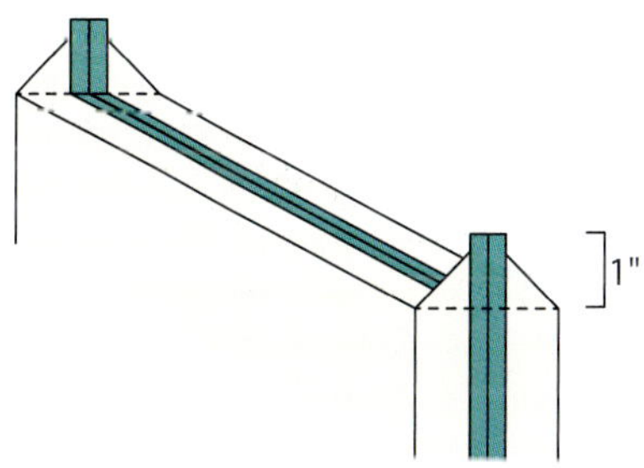

8. Turn bag right side out through opening; sew opening closed. Push lining into bag.
9. Tie ribbon through zipper pull; trim ends.

4-patch QUILT

Finished Quilt Size: $43\frac{1}{2}$" x $64\frac{3}{4}$" (110 cm x 164 cm)
Finished Block Size: $7\frac{1}{2}$" x $7\frac{1}{2}$" (19 cm x 19 cm)

SHOPPING LIST

Yardage is based on 43"/44" (109 cm/112 cm) wide fabric with a usable width of 40" (102 cm). Fat quarters are approximately 18" x 21" (46 cm x 53 cm).

- ☐ $2\frac{1}{2}$ yds (2.3 m) of purple solid fabric (includes binding)
- ☐ 6 assorted print fat quarters
- ☐ 52" x 73" (132 cm x 185 cm) piece of batting
- ☐ $4\frac{1}{8}$ yds (3.8 m) of fabric for backing

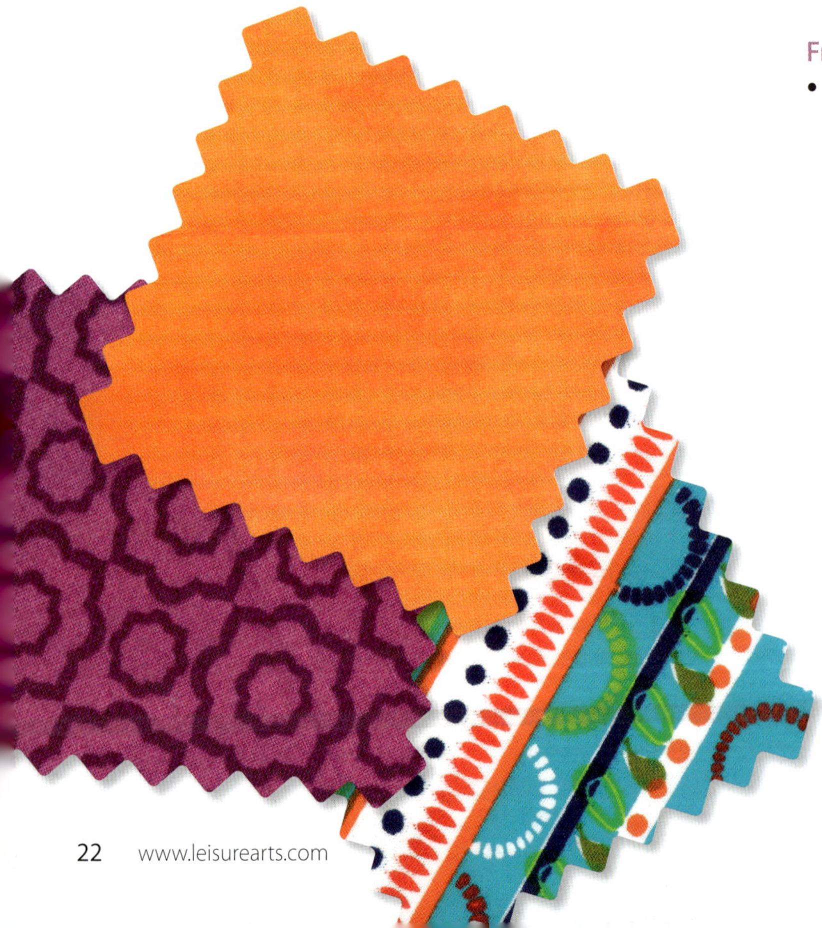

CUTTING THE PIECES

*Follow **Rotary Cutting**, page 26, to cut fabric. For yardage, cut all strips from the selvage-to-selvage width of the fabric. For fat quarters, cut all strips parallel to the long edge of the fabric. The setting triangles are cut slightly larger and will be trimmed after stitching. All measurements include $\frac{1}{4}$" seam allowances.*

From purple solid fabric:

- Cut 2 strips 12" wide. From these strips, cut 4 squares 12" x 12". Cut each square in half ***twice*** diagonally to make a total of 16 **large setting triangles**.
- From remainder of strip, cut 2 squares $6\frac{1}{4}$" x $6\frac{1}{4}$". Cut each square in half ***once*** diagonally to make a total of 4 **small setting triangles**.
- Cut 14 strips 3" wide. From these strips, cut 39 **large rectangles** 3" x 8" and 39 **small rectangles** 3" x $5\frac{1}{2}$".
- Cut 6 **binding strips** $2\frac{1}{4}$" wide.

From *each* assorted print fat quarter:

- Cut 5 strips 3" wide. From these strips, cut a total of 30 **squares** 3" x 3". (You will have extra squares. This will provide variety in your blocks.)

JANE AUSTEN

MAKING THE BLOCK

*Follow **Machine Sewing or Piecing**, page 27, and **Pressing**, page 28, to complete quilt. Match right sides and raw edges and use a $^{1}/_{4}$" seam allowance throughout.*

1. Sew 2 assorted **squares** together to make **Unit 1**. Make 78 Unit 1's. Sew 2 Unit 1's together to make **Unit 2**. Make 39 Unit 2's. Unit 2's should measure 5$^{1}/_{2}$" x 5$^{1}/_{2}$" including seam allowances.

Unit 1 (make 78)

Unit 2 (make 39)

2. Sew 1 **small rectangle** to each Unit 2 to make **Unit 3**. Make 39 Unit 3's. Sew 1 **large rectangle** to each Unit 3 to make a **Block**. Make 39 Blocks. Blocks should measure 8" x 8" including seam allowances.

Unit 3 (make 39)

Block (make 39)

ASSEMBLING THE QUILT TOP

*Refer to **Assembly Diagram** to assemble quilt top.*

1. Aligning 1 edge, stitch **Blocks** and **large setting triangles** together in diagonal rows. Press seam allowances in alternating directions.
2. Nesting seam allowances, stitch the diagonal rows together.
3. Centering the triangle on the Block, stitch a **small setting triangle** to each corner. Press the seam allowances toward the Blocks.
4. Trim the quilt top to 43" x $64^{1}/_{4}$".

FINISHING THE QUILT

1. Follow **Quilting**, page 28, to mark, layer, and quilt as desired. Our quilt is quilted with an all-over meandering pattern.
2. Sew binding strips together end to end; press seam allowances open. Follow **Binding**, page 30, to bind quilt.

Assembly Diagram

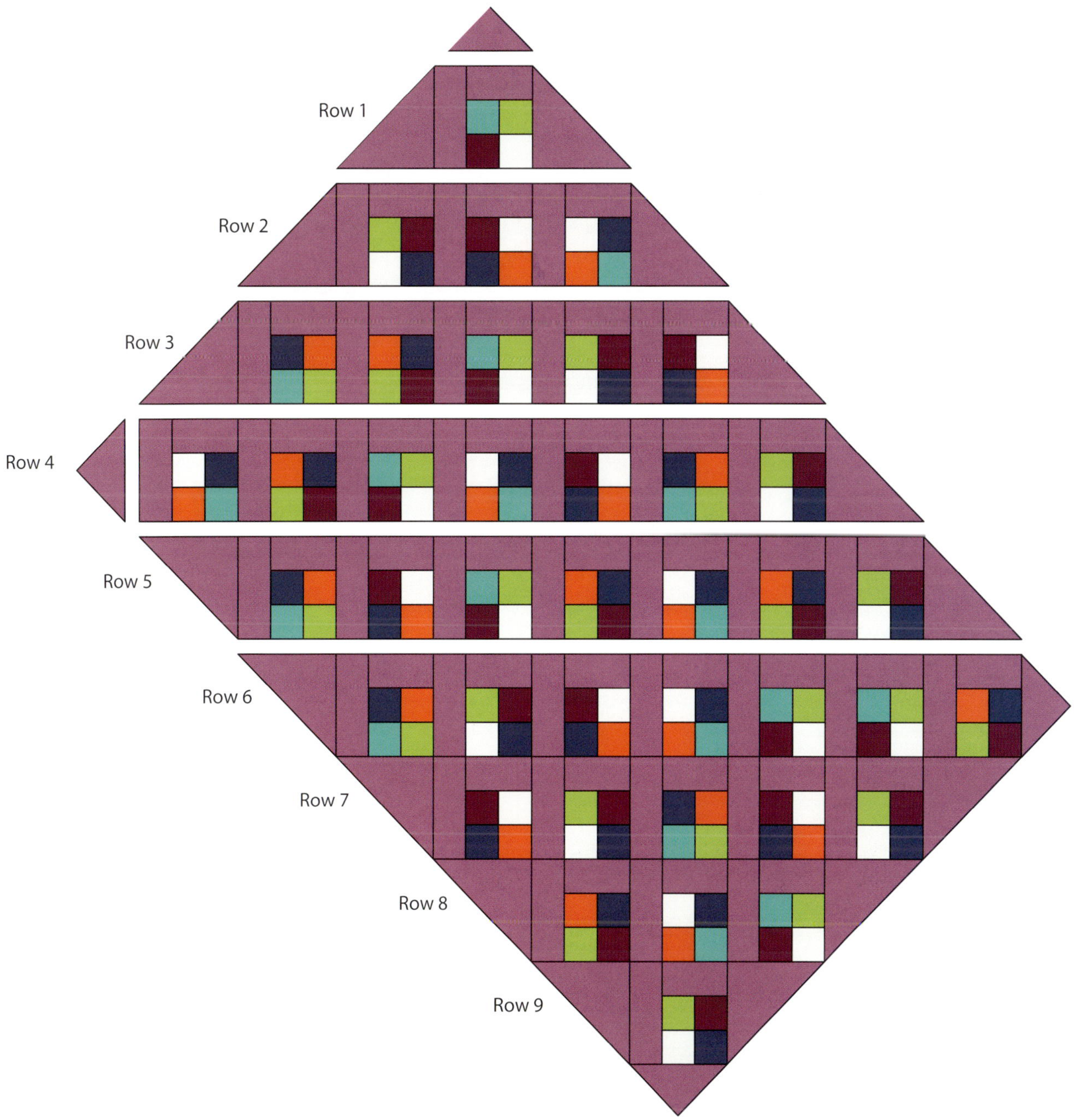

general INSTRUCTIONS

To make your project easier and more enjoyable, we encourage you to carefully read all of the general instructions, study the color photographs, and familiarize yourself with the individual project instructions before beginning.

FABRICS

SELECTING FABRICS

Choose high-quality, medium-weight 100% cotton fabrics. All-cotton fabrics hold a crease better, fray less, and are easier to quilt than cotton/polyester blends.

Yardage requirements listed for each project are based on 43"/44" wide fabric with a "usable" width of 40" after shrinkage and trimming selvages. Actual usable width will probably vary slightly from fabric to fabric. Our recommended yardage lengths should be adequate for occasional re-squaring of fabric when many cuts are required.

PREPARING FABRICS

Pre-washing fabrics may cause edges to ravel. As a result, your precut fabrics may not be large enough to cut all of the pieces required for your chosen project. Therefore, we do not recommend pre-washing yardage or precut fabrics.

Before cutting, prepare fabrics with a steam iron set on cotton and starch or sizing. The starch or sizing will give the fabric a crisp finish. This will make cutting more accurate and may make piecing easier.

ROTARY CUTTING

CUTTING FROM YARDAGE

- Place fabric on work surface with fold closest to you.
- Cut all strips from the selvage-to-selvage width of the fabric unless otherwise indicated in project instructions.

- Square left edge of fabric using rotary cutter and rulers **(Figs. 1-2)**.

Fig. 1

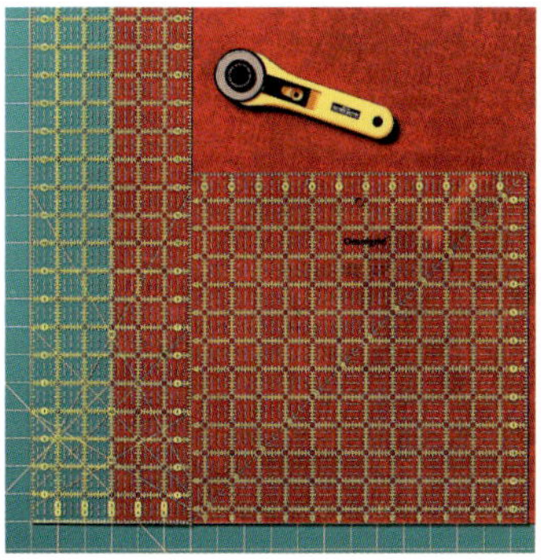

Fig. 2

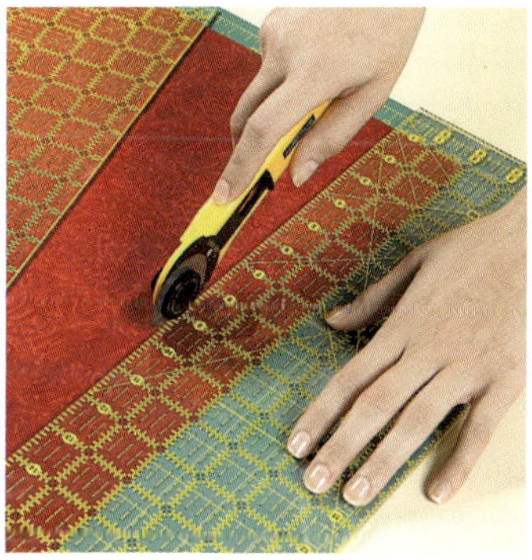

- To cut each strip required for a project, place ruler over cut edge of fabric, aligning desired marking on ruler with cut edge; make cut **(Fig. 3)**.

Fig. 3

- When cutting several strips from a single piece of fabric, it is important to make sure that cuts remain at a perfect right angle to the fold; square fabric as needed.

CUTTING FROM PRECUT FABRICS

- Place fabric flat on work surface with short edge closest to you.
- Square left long edge of fabric in the same manner as above.
- Cut all strips parallel to the long edge of the fabric.
- To cut each strip required for a project, place ruler over cut edge of fabric, aligning desired marking on ruler with cut edge; make cut.

MACHINE SEWING OR PIECING

Precise cutting, followed by accurate sewing, will ensure that all pieces of your project fit together well.

- Set sewing machine stitch length for approximately 11 stitches per inch.
- Use neutral-colored general-purpose sewing thread (not quilting thread) in needle and in bobbin.
- An accurate seam allowance is essential. Presser feet that are $^1/_4$" wide are available for most sewing machines. There are also guidelines on the machine that can be used to measure accurate seam allowance width.
- Always place pieces right sides together and match raw edges unless otherwise indicated; pin if necessary.
- Trim away points of seam allowances that extend beyond edges of sewn pieces.

SEWING ACROSS SEAM INTERSECTIONS

When sewing across intersection of two seams, place pieces right sides together and match seams exactly, making sure seam allowances are pressed in opposite directions **(Fig. 4)**.

Fig. 4

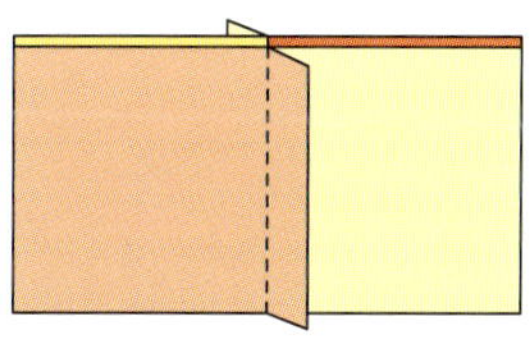

SEWING SHARP POINTS

To ensure sharp points when joining triangular or diagonal pieces, stitch across the center of the "X" (shown in pink) formed on wrong side by previous seams **(Fig. 5)**.

Fig. 5

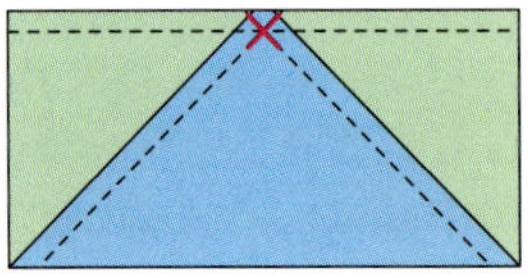

PRESSING

- Use steam iron set on "Cotton" for all pressing.
- Press after sewing each seam.
- Seam allowances are almost always pressed to one side, usually toward darker fabric. However, to reduce bulk it may occasionally be necessary to press seam allowances toward the lighter fabric or even to press them open.
- To prevent dark fabric seam allowance from showing through light fabric, trim darker seam allowance slightly narrower than lighter seam allowance.

QUILTING

Quilting holds the three layers (top, batting, and backing) of the quilt together and can be done by hand or machine. Because marking, layering, and quilting are interrelated and may be done in different orders depending on circumstances, please read entire Quilting section, pages 28-30, before beginning project.

TYPES OF QUILTING DESIGNS

In the Ditch Quilting

Quilting along seamlines or along edges of appliquéd pieces is called "in the ditch" quilting. This type of quilting should be done on side opposite seam allowance and does not have to be marked.

Channel Quilting

Quilting with straight, parallel lines is called "channel" quilting. This type of quilting may be marked or stitched using a guide.

Crosshatch Quilting

Quilting straight lines in a grid pattern is called "crosshatch" quilting. Lines may be stitched parallel to edges of quilt or stitched diagonally. This type of quilting may be marked or stitched using a guide.

Meandering Quilting

Quilting in random curved lines and swirls is called "meandering" quilting. Quilting lines should not cross or touch each other. This type of quilting does not need to be marked.

Stipple Quilting

Meandering quilting that is very closely spaced is called "stipple" quilting. Stippling will flatten the area quilted and is often stitched in background areas to raise appliquéd or pieced designs. This type of quilting does not need to be marked.

MARKING QUILTING LINES

Quilting lines may be marked using fabric marking pencils, chalk markers, or water- or air-soluble pens.

Simple quilting designs may be marked with chalk or chalk pencil after basting. A small area may be marked, then quilted, before moving to next area to be marked. Intricate designs should be marked before basting using a more durable marker.

Caution: Pressing may permanently set some marks. Test different markers on scrap fabric to find one that marks clearly and can be thoroughly removed.

PREPARING THE QUILT BACKING

To allow for slight shifting of quilt top during quilting, backing should be approximately 4" larger on all sides. Yardage requirements listed for quilt backings are calculated for 43"/44"w fabric. To piece a backing using 43"/44"w fabric, use the following instructions.

1. Measure length and width of quilt top; add 8" to each measurement.
2. Cut backing fabric into two lengths slightly longer than determined length measurement. Trim selvages. Place lengths with right sides facing and sew long edges together, forming tube **(Fig. 6)**. Match seams and press along one fold **(Fig. 7)**. Cut along pressed fold to form single piece **(Fig. 8)**.

Fig. 6

Fig. 7

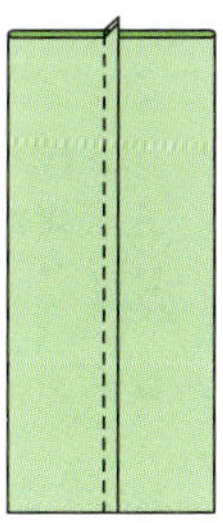

Fig. 8

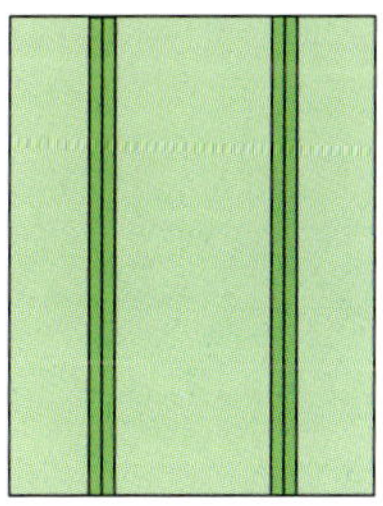

3. Trim backing to size determined in Step 1; press seam allowances open.

CHOOSING THE BATTING

The appropriate batting will make quilting easier. For fine hand quilting, choose low-loft batting. All cotton or cotton/polyester blend battings work well for machine quilting because the cotton helps "grip" quilt layers. If quilt is to be tied, a high-loft batting, sometimes called extra-loft or fat batting, may be used to make quilt "fluffy."

Types of batting include cotton, polyester, wool, silk, cotton/polyester blend, and cotton/wool blend.

When selecting batting, refer to package labels for characteristics and care instructions. Cut batting same size as prepared backing.

ASSEMBLING THE QUILT

1. Examine wrong side of quilt top closely; trim any seam allowances and clip any threads that may show through front of the quilt. Press quilt top, being careful not to "set" any marked quilting lines.
2. Place backing wrong side up on flat surface. Use masking tape to tape edges of backing to surface. Place batting on top of backing fabric. Smooth batting gently, being careful not to stretch or tear. Center quilt top right side up on batting.
3. Use 1" rustproof safety pins to "pin-baste" all layers together, spacing pins approximately 4" apart. Begin at center and work toward outer edges to secure all layers. If possible, place pins away from areas that will be quilted, although pins may be removed as needed when quilting.

MACHINE QUILTING METHODS

Use general-purpose thread in bobbin. Do not use quilting thread. Thread the needle of machine with general-purpose thread or transparent monofilament thread to make quilting blend with quilt top fabrics. Use decorative thread, such as a metallic or contrasting-color general-purpose thread, to make quilting lines stand out more.

Straight-Line Quilting

The term "straight-line" is somewhat deceptive, since curves (especially gentle ones) as well as straight lines can be stitched with this technique.

1. Set stitch length for six to ten stitches per inch and attach walking foot to sewing machine.
2. Determine which section of quilt will have longest continuous quilting line, often area from center top to center bottom. Roll up and secure each edge of quilt to help reduce the bulk, keeping fabrics smooth. Smaller projects may not need to be rolled.
3. Begin stitching on longest quilting line, using very short stitches for the first 1/4" to "lock" quilting. Stitch across project, using one hand on each side of walking foot to slightly spread fabric and to guide fabric through machine. Lock stitches at end of quilting line.
4. Continue machine quilting, stitching longer quilting lines first to stabilize quilt before moving on to other areas.

Free-Motion Quilting

Free-motion quilting may be free form or may follow a marked pattern.

1. Attach darning foot to sewing machine and lower or cover feed dogs.
2. Position quilt under darning foot; lower foot. Holding top thread, take a stitch and pull bobbin thread to top of quilt. To "lock" beginning of quilting line, hold top and bobbin threads while making three to five stitches in place.
3. Use one hand on each side of darning foot to slightly spread fabric and to move fabric through the machine. Even stitch length is achieved by using smooth, flowing hand motion and steady machine speed. Slow machine speed and fast hand movement will create long stitches. Fast machine speed and slow hand movement will create short stitches. Move quilt sideways, back and forth, in a circular motion, or in a random motion to create desired designs; do not rotate quilt. Lock stitches at end of each quilting line.

BINDING

ATTACHING BINDING WITH MITERED CORNERS

1. Beginning with one end near center on bottom edge of quilt, lay binding around quilt to make sure that seams in binding will not end up at a corner. Adjust placement if necessary. Matching raw edges of binding to raw edge of quilt top, pin binding to right side of quilt along one edge.
2. When you reach first corner, mark 1/4" from corner of quilt top **(Fig. 9)**.

Fig. 9

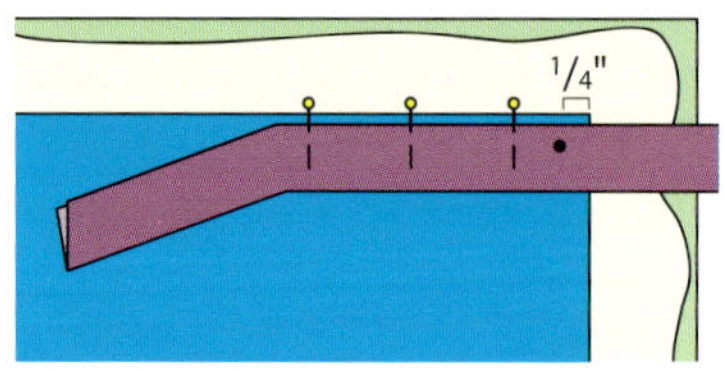

3. Beginning approximately 10" from end of binding and using a 1/4" seam allowance, sew binding to quilt, backstitching at beginning of stitching and at mark **(Fig. 10)**. Lift needle out of fabric and clip thread.

Fig. 10

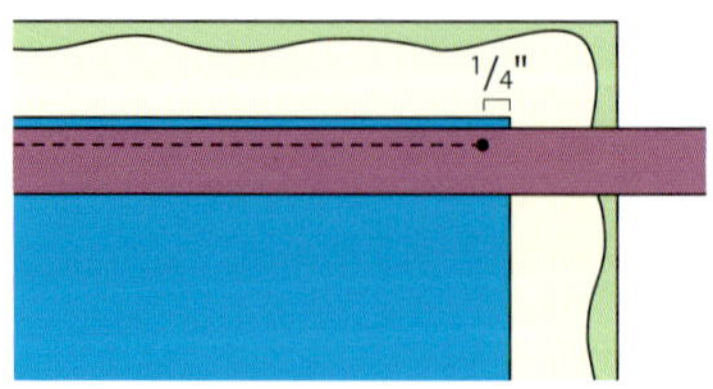

4. Fold binding as shown in **Figs. 11-12** and pin binding to adjacent side, matching raw edges. When you've reached the next corner, mark 1/4" from edge of quilt top.

Fig. 11

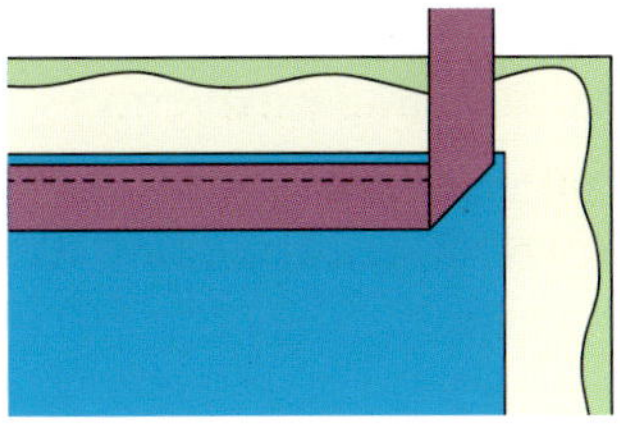

Fig. 12

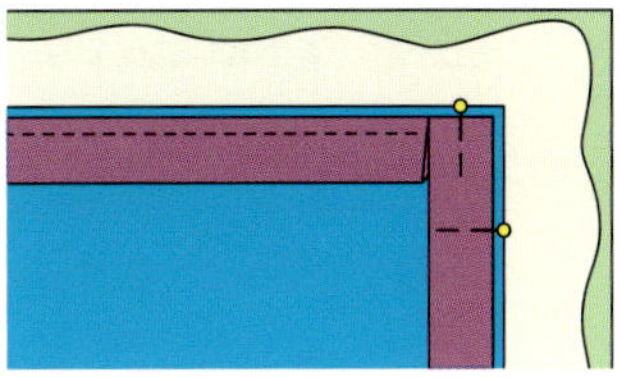

5. Backstitching at edge of quilt top, sew pinned binding to quilt **(Fig. 13)**; backstitch at the next mark. Lift needle out of fabric and clip thread.

Fig. 13

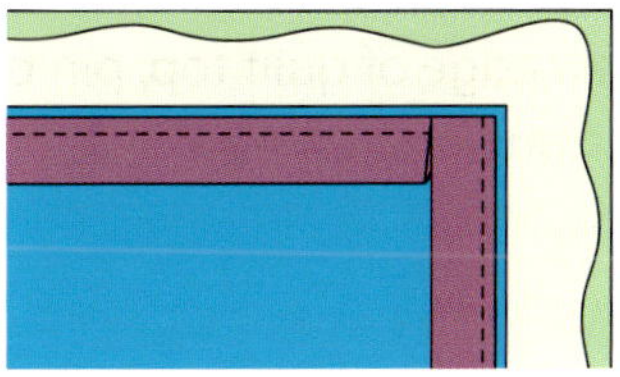

6. Continue sewing binding to quilt, stopping approximately 10" from starting point **(Fig. 14)**.

Fig. 14

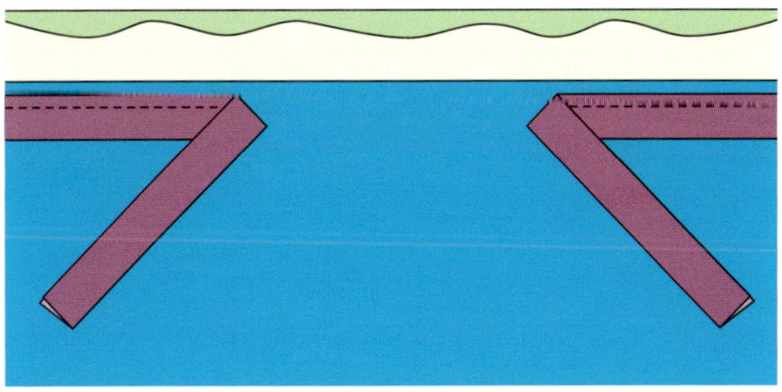

7. Bring beginning and end of binding to center of opening and fold each end back, leaving a 1/4" space between folds **(Fig. 15)**. Finger press folds.

Fig. 15

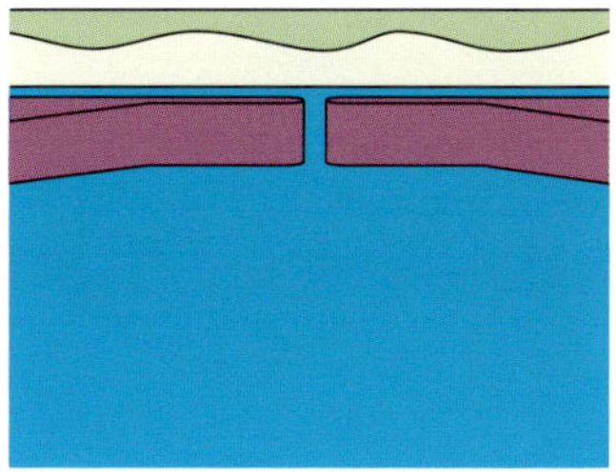

8. Unfold ends of binding and draw a line across wrong side in finger-pressed crease. Draw a line through the lengthwise pressed fold of binding at the same spot to create a cross mark. With edge of ruler at cross mark, line up 45° angle marking on ruler with one long side of binding. Draw a diagonal line from edge to edge. Repeat on remaining end, making sure that the two diagonal lines are angled the same way **(Fig. 16)**.

Fig. 16

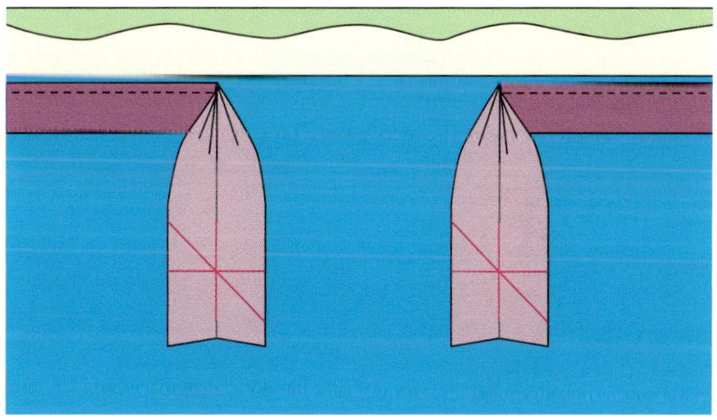

9. Matching right sides and diagonal lines, pin binding ends together at right angles **(Fig. 17)**.

Fig. 17

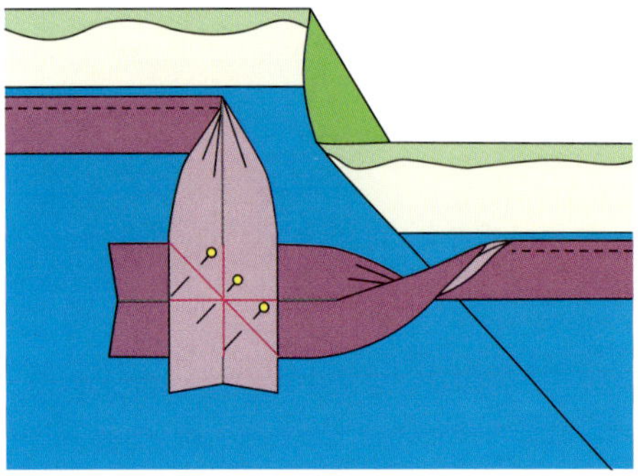

10. Machine stitch along diagonal line **(Fig. 18)**, removing pins as you stitch.

Fig. 18

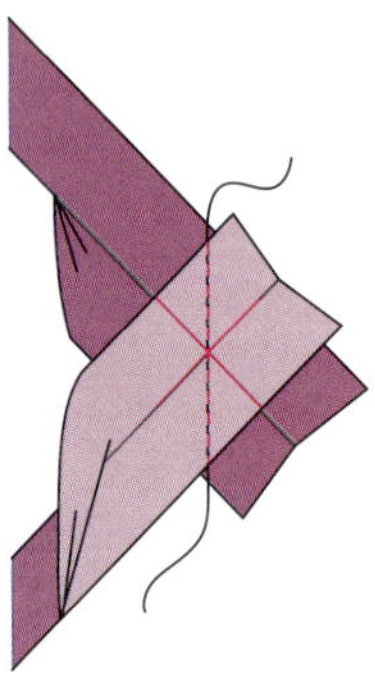

11. Lay binding against quilt to double check that it is correct length.
12. Trim binding ends, leaving 1/4" seam allowance; press seam open. Stitch binding to quilt.
13. Trim backing and batting even with edges of quilt top.
14. On one edge of quilt, fold binding over to quilt backing and pin pressed edge in place, covering stitching line **(Fig. 19)**. On adjacent side, fold binding over, forming a mitered corner **(Fig. 20)**. Repeat to pin remainder of binding in place.

Fig. 19

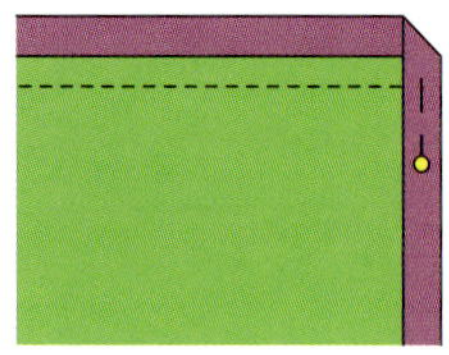

Fig. 20

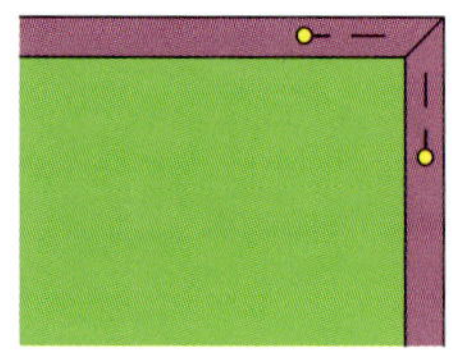

15. Blindstitch binding to backing, taking care not to stitch through to front of quilt.

Metric Conversion Chart

Inches x 2.54 = centimeters (cm)	Yards x .9144 = meters (m)
Inches x 25.4 = millimeters (mm)	Yards x 91.44 = centimeters (cm)
Inches x .0254 = meters (m)	Centimeters x .3937 = inches (")
	Meters x 1.0936 = yards (yd)

Standard Equivalents

1/8"	3.2 mm	0.32 cm	1/8 yard	11.43 cm	0.11 m
1/4"	6.35 mm	0.635 cm	1/4 yard	22.86 cm	0.23 m
3/8"	9.5 mm	0.95 cm	3/8 yard	34.29 cm	0.34 m
1/2"	12.7 mm	1.27 cm	1/2 yard	45.72 cm	0.46 m
5/8"	15.9 mm	1.59 cm	5/8 yard	57.15 cm	0.57 m
3/4"	19.1 mm	1.91 cm	3/4 yard	68.58 cm	0.69 m
7/8"	22.2 mm	2.22 cm	7/8 yard	80 cm	0.8 m
1"	25.4 mm	2.54 cm	1 yard	91.44 cm	0.91 m

Many thanks to Delorse Richards for her beautiful sewing on the 4-Patch Quilt and to Eddie Landreth, the Arkansas Man Quilter, for his beautiful longarm machine quilting on the 4-Patch Quilt and Wild Goose Chase Table Runner.

Production Team: Designers – Lisa Lancaster and Kelly Reider; Technical Editor – Lisa Lancaster; Associate Editor – Mary Sullivan Hutcheson; Editorial Writer – Susan Frantz Wiles; Art Category Manager – Lora Puls; Graphic Artists – Frances Huddleston and Kellie McAnulty; Photography Stylist – Lori Wenger; Photographer – Jason Masters

Made In U.S.A